The Cry of

The Ravven

Ravven White

Curious Corvid
PUBLISHING

The Cry of The Ravven by Ravven White

Published by Curious Corvid Publishing, LLC.

Copyright © 2022 by Ravven White

Cover design by Rad Studio, LLC © 2021, Mitch Green

Printed in the United States of America

Cataloging-in-Publication Data is on file with the Library of Congress.

ISBN: 979-8-9855940-9-6
Also available on Kindle
www.curiouscorvidpublishing.com

For SeeJay

You're familiar,
Like my mirror years ago…

Hello my loves,

It has been a while since last we spoke. We shared a moment over my previous collection – my goodness has time flown by. So much has changed. So much has grown. I often wonder of you and how you are doing. I hope you are loving yourself, completely, and finding ways to pursue your happiness. I'm a firm believer that if more people pursued their passions, their happiness would spill into the world and make it that much lovelier.

In my last collection, I Am Ravven, I tried to give you a peek into where it was that I came from. A small look into why I am the way I am and the life I've tried to build for myself. I wish that such things were more pleasant and that I had lovely memories to share over a steaming cup of hot tea in one of my many gardens.

Yes, many gardens. Some gardens are monuments to memories, some are shrines to lost loves, current loves, even loves yet to be. Some are resting places for you, my dear readers, to rest your weary wings in. There is magic and mystery in moonlight gardens and this heart of mine has planted many...

But I wasn't always traipsing about a green forest and making delicious tea.

You see, my loves, when I wrote *I Am Ravven*, it ended with a taste of freedom after isolation. A promise of something better after devastation. A moonbeam in an eternal dark. A garden in a desolate land.

But freedom always comes at a cost.

I want you to know that no matter where you are, no matter where you have come from, there is always a chance for something better and there is always a choice for healing. Even in our darkest moments when all seems lost and our heart is broken, we have a choice. But it isn't always easy. Sometimes, holding on for the healing hurts the most. Sometimes the night we choose to stay alive is the darkest and the longest.

So, I wish to share with you what happened when the lost girl chose to become 'Ravven'.

When she finally spoke her story and began her descent into the darkness. When her questions and chaos kept her awake and stole her sanity. When it hurt so, so much that her heart felt like it would never be healed.

I think it's important to keep an honest and realistic approach to healing. When we decide to take that step and make ourselves better, it's a lot of work. Things don't get better overnight (though how wonderful that would be). I don't ever want to present the idea that healing is a piece of cake. Mmm, cake. Let's have cake at the next get together. Anyway, sometimes it takes a while and sometimes it's hard.

I bounced around doing different things to heal myself for a long time. I had a therapist, briefly, and got out of the habit of going. Plus, it was easier to just not talk about the sadness and hurt. I made progress on my own but after Link (my husband) and I were blessed with our daughter Starlight, I knew I couldn't let the cycle of trauma continue. I found myself a therapist I could trust and took the cold plunge into the depths of my heart. I remember during my first session feeling so raw and vulnerable, tears streaming down my cheeks as I asked my therapist the most burning question on my mind:

"Will it always hurt this much?"
"It doesn't have to." She replied.

And she was right. I want to show you my fight for the sun to give you encouragement as you fight for yours. You can do it, you absolutely can my loves. You have no idea the glory and life that is waiting for you on the other side of your hurt. There is hope, always. Don't let go. Promise me you won't, I would miss you terribly.

Well, I should wrap up this letter if I am to ever get it off to you. I'm sending you love, and healing, and lovely gardens, and warm cups of tea. You will find me here, in my moonlit gardens, scribbling my crazed poetry and talking to my corvids. Have you seen a corvid lately? They always seem to show up when I'm having a bad day. I extend that to you – if you see a crow or a raven, chances are I have sent them to you to remind you that it's going to be okay.

Take care, dear readers, and keep looking for your sun. It is there.

We will talk soon!

Love always,
Ravven

The Legend of The White Raven

A Retelling

Once upon a time

Oh, so many a moon ago,

The world was bathed in a darkness

Unlike any that we know.

You may think we know of shadows,

Of darkness, and of night,

But the world was once cold and desolate

Ruled by an endless night.

There was no thriving and no living

Just existing to survive.

Monsters roamed this nightfall

Slaying all who were alive.

Growls danced with darkness,

Pointed teeth flayed tender flesh –

In this world there was no safety

As the smell of blood hung fresh.

But not all the creatures were savage –

Some were wise and even kind

And they longed for warmth and for sunlight

But over time even they fell, resigned.

Hush now and listen my darlings

And I will tell you how our world came to be:

The legend of the White Raven

And how she altered our destiny…

Without sun there would not be plant life,

So in this world there was no lush green.

Only sparse, thorny shrubs grew in the ground

No moss, no flowers, no trees.

The birds of this world lived in mountains,

In high peaks coated in snow

And among these flocks lived the white ravens

(not the black ones that we now know).

They were regarded as Guardians,

A flash of white in the night –

They scouted the monsters most savage

And helped lesser creatures survive.

But even their numbers grew fewer

As the coldness crept into their bones

The monsters were growing much bolder

Invading the high peaks, their home.

One day every year the brutes cowered

When strange light pierced through the clouds.

Warmth and light flooded the atmosphere

And for this one day, no fear was allowed.

One White Raven dreamed of the sunlight,

Of endless days filled with hope.

Where all could live in their freedom,

Where all could be safe in their home.

The others forbade her from dreaming

"We are destined a duty to fill.

You can't save the world from the nightfall

For this is the way and the will."

So she soared in the night hunting monsters

A Guardian in this bleak place

But still she would dream of a sunlit world

Where freedom reflected her face…

One day she soared past the mountains

High into the atmosphere

She broke past the clouds and the gloominess

She felt freedom and safety, no fear.

And there, in the sky, shining brightly

Glowed a radiant beacon of hope

But it sat too far off in the distance

To reach the White Raven's home.

Quite suddenly, a crazy thought struck her:

What if…what if they flew to this sun

Grabbed hold of the rays with their talons

And render their nightfall undone?

With a heart beating wild and hopeful

She dove down back to her kin

And she told them the story of stealing the sun

And how she thought they should begin.

"Silence!" Echoed the elders

"Have you yet to learn your own place?

This is the last strike, be gone from our flock
You are an outcast and a disgrace!"
(And now you may know, my darlings,
Why flocks of ravens are called an Unkindness –
Forsaking their own and living in fear
Content with the dark and the violence.)
Abandoned by family and left to her own
The White Raven flew back to the sun
And she cried for the loss of her kin and home,
For the darkness and all that was done.
And when the tears dried from her clear eyes,
She straightened her feathers and head.
"I'll be the one to move the sun in the sky
For it is better than accepting the dead!"
Faster than whispers caught in the wind,
Our White Raven flew towards the light.
She would not give in to the heartache within,
She would not give into the night.
Wrapping her talons 'round flaming rays
She cried out as they burned to her bones

Her wingtips on fire as she started her flight

To bring hope back to her home.

Bearing light is a burden as all of us know

But the White Raven, she would not stop

Even as feathers blackened across her back

And her heart flickered between on and off.

Her kin heard her cries and soared to the sky

To see a flaming black bird bearing the sun.

In silence and awe they bore witness to her

And the miracle of all she had done.

They flew to her side and aided her feat

As the clouds parted and the darkness gave way,

And the earth was flooded in a gentle light

With the birth of the first day.

The monsters and creatures scurried away

Deep into caverns and caves.

As far from the light as they could hide,

Invading the earth and the waves.

The ravens, once Guardians of ancient night

Now flew mottled in black from the burns

Our White Raven, well she suffered the most –

She knew her white feathers would not return.

The earth heaved a sigh, warmed by the light

And felt the loss echo deep in her heart

But our Raven knew her job was not done,

And a new order is what she would start.

Behold, the mighty black ravens!

Guardians of wisdom and time!

They would go on to serve kingdoms and gods

For it is courage that runs in their line.

But once in a while, and somewhat rare

A white raven is born to an Unkindness.

A beautiful symbol of sacrifice

Left behind to forever remind us.

May we all be as brave as the White Raven

Who brought us the sun and the light,

Who refused to accept the way that things were

And chose hope over fear of the night.

Corvid Content

THE TRANSFORMATION   145

THE SUN   197

The Wound

My heart is stuck

In between

What could have been

And what should be.

Do You Remember?

I sometimes wonder if you even remember.

Do you play it over in your mind?

Do you hear me cry?

Probably not.

I don't remember crying the first time.

I remember dissociating the second time.

I remember wondering,

If I cut off my hand, will it stop burning?

Will I feel less sinful?

That's a heavy thought for a seven-year-old.

For any year-old.

I've never been able to look at my hand the same way.

It became diseased on that horrible day.

Do you know what I've done to purify it?

As if I was to blame for it.

I thought it only happened a few times

But the brain makes up its own lies

And it turns out, you stole *years*.

I sometimes wish I could cry those tears,

The ones that welled up

As I prayed and begged that you would just stop.

- *please stop. please stop. please stop.* -

But you didn't. Not once. Not ever.

And then you had the nerve to call me *daughter.*

I prayed and prayed for someone to save me

But no one ever came to save me

And I was left with daydreaming

Of slitting wrists and losing hands.

I am sick to think that you remember.

I am sick that I remember.

I am sick that I don't remember.

Power

I remember the day I realized
What power really felt like.
He called me over to the bathroom
Where he was mending holes.
Ironic since he was always making holes –
Or raping holes in hearts, in bodies –
And he beckoned me, smiling,
Before raising a 2x4 and striking
My small, eight-year-old body.
I braced against the sink,
Stunned, eyes watering,
My child mind racing.
"Do you know why I did that?" He asked.
I shook my head.

He smiled, again.

"Because I could."

I braced for impact.

Four Letter Words

I have spent the last four days consumed by a four-
letter word
As if the brand on my body heard it and burned,
And I have been lost in a darkness I did not deserve
to revisit -
A frightened child abused, beaten, locked in a closet.
I write in riddles and secrets that hedge around
darkness,
And it burns me alive as my grief smolders,
boundless.
But I saw a comment that seared me to my soul
And I wonder, is this what the world thinks it knows?
"Rape isn't akin to death. Sounds to me a bit
dramatic."
So flippant. So easy to just disregard it.
And this, this is the word scarred on my skin
That destroys me alive, without and within.
In what way could rape never be anything but death,
As we are smothered and silenced, holding our
breath?

It's a death and passing of what could have been -
A death of the safety that should have been,
A death of living, replaced with survival
A death of peace, of hope, of revival
Because who we were before cannot ever return
And we are left in the aftermath, unmarked graves,
ashen urns.
Tell me, tell me that I'm being dramatic,
That I got to live – I got to live through it,
But I have to live with this sin and you don't
You say you understand but I know that you won't.
This disgraceful commentary diminishes rape
And the terrible things born of that place
We must acknowledge the destruction and pain,
That rape is an action, not just a name.
It should be treated as death, a loss of sweet life –
I may be living but I'm not quite right.
You don't just "come back" once it happens to you,
It takes courage and strength to start over brand new,
To say goodbye to who you were and what could
have been,
Like safety, security, trust in women and men.
And I just want you to know, if it's happened to you,

You're not alone and I'm walking with you

And I acknowledge your pain, your destruction, your end

And I will help you scatter your ashes into the wind.

Death cannot stop us, I have never believed it

But I promise to you, I will always acknowledge it.

So I will share this small piece, just let it sink in:

I died that day.

And the next day.

And again.

And again.

Happy Endings

Some days I am reminded
Of all the ways I am not good enough.
They surround me like bullies to a child
Taunting me, teasing me,
Throwing words, and sticks, and stones at me.
These bullies represent my own insecurities:
My womb, my weight, my mediocrity,
The kind of friendships that will never be,
A heart labeled 'level 10 catastrophe'.
All these ways I can just never be good enough.

I suppose if I can never be good enough,
I will just have to be good.
Be what I would.
Speak as I should.
Love as I could.
That is all I have.
I would like my poetry
To always wrap up positively
Bittersweet hope intermingled lovingly

But not this time,

Not these lines.

In keeping with this sentiment,

This poem will not be good enough

It's not good enough.

Not good enough.

Not good enough

For a happy ending.

Heart Measurements

When I was younger,
I was taller and stronger
Than my counterparts.
Somehow, being stronger
Translated into 'larger'.
But in truth, I was just developing faster.
With a tall frame
And developed muscles,
I was deemed less feminine
And more manly.
Less to be admired or desired,
And more to be criticized.
"You are so much bigger than
Everyone else!"
And I was.
But I never understood
Why 'bigger' was bad,
Why my height and strength
Were considered less feminine
Why I was 'less than'

Compared to my smaller,

Shorter, more feminine friends.

Being 'bigger' was a negative.

I didn't understand

What the adults meant

When they sneered it,

So, I took it to mean

That 'bigger' and 'larger'

Automatically meant 'fatter'.

In grade school I had to sit

At the back of the class

Because I was the tallest.

The boys called me 'freak'

I didn't know I made them feel insecure,

All I knew is that everyone

Said I was 'bigger'.

My aunt halved my food

On every visit

Regardless of portion or the size of it

And my stepfather told me

I needed to watch my weight

So I could someday bear children.

I think you can see where this might be going…

By teenage years came my developing fears

I came into a body virtually overnight

I was mortified when my mother

Took me to the store

To buy bigger bras and underwear.

My friends didn't need to worry

About their bodies –

They were still so small and petite.

I was tall with strong legs and arms

With a body of a woman

By age fourteen.

This concept of being 'bigger'

And 'larger'

Was a constant reminder

That my body was not one to be desired.

I look back now and realize

I was healthy, and I was perfect,

But that teenage girl never knew it.

If you know me,

You know my story

You know that I have a history

Of abuse and neglect,

Of childhood violation

So, you can only imagine

What happens next –

A young girl with a body she can't understand,

And a monster with nothing

But time and blood on his hands.

If I didn't have enough reasons

To hate my body before,

You can be sure

That I had plenty now.

Mix this all up,

And you've got a terrified girl

Labeled 'bigger with a body'

Scarred by years of history

And the lesson to be learned

Was that bodies like mine

Aren't meant to be loved

And if you're bigger than the world,

You. Will. Be. Hurt.

I became so disassociated from my body,

I began to neglect it,

I hurt it on purpose

And I became 'bigger'.

I became the thing everyone called me

And while the sadness

Was crushing me,

Food changed from

Sustenance to weaponry.

When I tell you, I step on the scale

To weigh my depression,

It's not a euphemism

It's to distract your attention

From the idea that I'm 'bigger'.

Now, I'm not blaming all those numbers

On my huge history,

I know when I should take credit for misery

But I'll be honest,

It started in my innocence

It started when I was just a little kid.

My body was not created equal,

In fact, I don't know

A single one that is,

So, to compare and resize

Is a travesty in my eyes

Because if you're strong and you're healthy,

That should be good enough for you.

It should be good for everyone else, too.

The one thing I can say is: It's true, I am bigger.

But I measure by my heart

Not by my hips,

I measure by the words

That spill from my lips,

I measure by the poetry

I write with my hands,

I measure with the love

No one else understands.

It's taken me twenty-seven years

To realize I was bigger in their eyes

But I have grown into my body

And into my life

And I must admit,

My heart is too large

To be measured or defined.

'Bigger' is not always a bad thing.

'Larger' is not always a bad thing,

Love is the only thing

That makes the body worthy

To keep on pumping

It's beautiful beating heart.

When it comes down to it,

There are worse things than being 'fat'.
Maybe I've gotten off track
But the message I hope you take from this
Is to educate your children
To be strong and healthy,
Teach them that their heart
Should be the biggest part
Of their bodies,
Make sure they know
They can be larger than life
Whether they are short or tall
Whether they are black or white.
Teach them that food
Is a pleasurable responsibility
And that care of their body
Is a personal priority
And that when they gaze into the mirror
They feel love and beauty
Not shame and hate
Over someone else's unnecessary commentary.
There's enough hate in this world to crush them.
Don't let that hate begin
With you.

My Heart Hurts Today

I stood in the trees and screamed.

Or at least I tried to,

I never learned how to scream

I was always told to be silent.

Shh. It doesn't hurt that bad.

I stood in the trees and screamed

There were tears there,

They were streaming.

I was unaware they were dripping,

Because I was focused on screaming.

There was no sound as I sobbed into a blue sky

Cloudless, even,

A template of everything I wasn't.

My throat was raw from this soundless scream.

I imagine the words came out bloody

Because it felt like they tore right through me.

I stood in the trees and screamed.

I screamed for all the things I lost,

For all the time it cost,

For moments stolen from me

Replaced with sordid memories,

For every love affair my broken heart

Has tried to resuscitate,

For this wealth of emotions

That I so desperately hate.

For days like this day

When there are no words left to say,

Just screams,

Because it is suddenly

So overwhelming.

Knowing I can't have the normal things

Because this war was thrust upon me.

It's up to me to do the bloodletting

And I...

Well, I am in so much pain

All I'm left with is screaming.

At least the neighbors couldn't hear me

Silent convulsions ripping through me...

I stood in the trees and screamed:

"Is it ever

Going to be okay?"

Pink

I knew I was different.

He forced me to smother it.

Their worship condemned it.

I thought I deserved it.

I thought *he* is what caused it.

I tried to hide it.

I tried to swallow it.

I self-destructed attempting to stop it.

Purple

I just wanted to be good enough –
Perfect girl with perfect grades
A less than pretty, perfect face
But who needs pretty when the soul is empty?
A holy girl beloved by many.
Gentle spirit, quiet soul
- no one knew just what he stole –
You read your Bible, you did your chores.
You were thankful and never asked for more.
But you fantasized of being whisked away
Being loved by many who always stayed
Of flowers, and sunsets, and gentle kisses
While you washed the laundry and dirty dishes.
A tender heart with so much love to give
With crushes that you thought were sins.
I just wanted to be good enough –
Good enough to just be loved.

Blue

'Tis a delicate dance
To be caught betwixt two –
Hiding the colors
That would expose you.
Pushing through panic
As lust courts with love,
Seduced by hellfire
Claimed from above…

Attention Whore

I gaze at her, unquestioningly.
She gazes back, hauntingly.

She says she does not want to go on
And that she's all run out of commas
I reply that I'm tired of her and dealing with all her
drama.
She whispers that sometimes when she's driving,
She thinks of running off the road.
I tell her that attention whores are really getting old.
She mentions that she's stopped eating
After stepping on the scale.
I tell her she reminds me of a bloated, floating whale.
Sometimes she says she is depressed and wishes it
away
I respond that she really has no reasons to complain.
She says she has anxiety about being all alone.
I convince her that she's become too attached to her
phone.
She cries to me at midnight hours

That her dreams have gotten bad.

I tell her she needs to grow up, that her act is really sad.

She begs me on her broken knees to take her life away.

I coolly close my eyes, my heart, and coldly walk away.

She looks at me with bloody eyes

From staying up too late.

I tell her to use eyedrops to flush the dark away.

She tries to speak, to beg for love

And I slap her in the face.

I scream that there's no love for such an empty waste of space.

I grab a fistful of her hair

And make ger gaze into my eyes

"You're a pathetic excuse for a human being –

You're lucky I keep you alive!"

I throw her into a tiny room locked with a bleeding key

And I leave her there and walk away

As she screams, "Please set me free!"

Only once she's quiet and well contained

Will I grace her presence more
And she'll humbly thank me for keeping her in check,
My little attention whore.

I gaze at her, unquestioningly.
She gazes back, hauntingly.

I should really clean the mirror.

Psalms

Cages and broken places
Little girl with many faces
Creating joy with imagination
Freedom from her isolation
- I wonder -
When you sang psalms
From your worn-out Bible,
Did you know that someday,
You'd be the lamp upon the table?
In the darkness we are surrounded
By broken vessels beneath bruises
And it's true, you were the target
For a plethora of abuses.
Isolated and alone,
Did you have no love to call your own?
- I wonder -
Did your days blend together
Like the colors on your skin?
Or are your memories still hidden
And buried deep within?

It's a sin, and there are many

As days become your memories,

As you sang psalms from your Bible

Because those passages meant *everything*.

- I wonder -

Did you know that you were dying?

Singing psalms of times so trying

And yet, singing psalms of joys and happiness

Of God's eternal faithfulness

Little Ravven, singing in your cage.

I have yet to know

How much of my graveyard you will take.

But oh, those days,

Little Corvid trapped in suffocation

With a soul that could not be broken

A subtle joy in psalms softly whispered

Prayers of desperation…

- I wonder -

Did you even know what you were praying for?

God knows your temple was defiled

And you were just a child

Singing psalms out of your Bible

In a cage so isolating,

A world mapped out on your skin,

And a heart breaking from within

A lock on the door, separating

You from everything you knew

Pretending you were okay

So your brothers wouldn't fear for you.

Are there any words

Encapsulating

Your experience in this place?

No.

How could there be?

To this day,

There is fear, and pain, and panic

A sickening by-product

Of keeping Corvids locked in cages

And little girls with many faces.

- I wonder -

Throughout this abomination

You had hope and determination

And that is what I wish to take from this:

That even as a child,

You would not fall sick

From this poisonous prison
You would live on
And you would beat him.
I will take a psalm to carry with me
My whole entire life
And I, a Ravven with many faces,
Will not forget these places
And I will not forget those bruises
I will never forget the abuses
And I will never forget
That I survived all of it.
Still, now at twenty-nine
I sometimes feel as though I
Am still locked in my tiny room
Because, this is what trauma does to you
And so, I whisper psalms:
"There is surely a future hope for you,
And your hope
Will not be cut off."

Burned Out Sun

I don't often speak
Of my days in the cage
I liken it as the days
The sun ceased to burn
A new kind of darkness
Of which I would learn
And life just grew cold
And stark…alone.
Locked inside of a cage
That became my new home.
So young and so tender
All boarded up
My closet deadbolted
My windows screwed shut.
No access to objects
Just enough clothes to cover up
Bread on my plate, water in my cup.
Bruises that he bequeathed me each day
My days were quite bleak
With no sun, just…gray.

And that's where he kept me
And forced me to stay.
I ate in this cage,
I slept in this cage
And I oft would be left in my waste
In this cage.
And he tried to break me
Oh, he tried very hard,
Denying me everything
Except for the rod
In a purgatory of pain
That had not an end.
Day after day after day that would blend.
The sun clouded out from all of the rain
As I watched the seasons
From my sealed windowpane.
But I was a spirit that
Could not be contained
And I would not be broken
By this tortuous cage.
But I don't often speak
Of this time in my life
It hurts to speak of it,

Even after all of this time.

Life needs sunshine

And in this place,

There was none

And so I am still trying

To look back and find some

In a place left cold

From a burned-out sun.

Just Another Late-Night Raving

I have a confession to make
As I lay here in bed
At a time far too late
For me to be awake
And yet, here I am.
I have always felt forgotten.
There. I have finally said it.
I know it sounds kind of selfish
But please bear with me
As I dissect this.
Growing up in a large family,
Of which I was the oldest,
Meant I was by default,
The strongest,
I was the bravest,
And, by trauma,
The loneliest.
I have always felt overlooked.
When it came to my siblings,
Lines were drawn at an early age

'Favorites' became a word I would hate

Along with my borderline existence

Because if existence is built

On consciousness,

I felt as though I was only

Relying on one:

My own.

Being the strongest in a family of abused

Meant taking my cue

To stand at the *back* of the line

Because if someone needed saving,

I would be there to save them.

Being the strongest take a toll

But it's okay when there is no one to notice

You are alone.

I know what this sounds like,

Like a self-righteous whining

But I have been waiting

To be noticed by my family.

Growing up in a broken home

Means someone must be the one

Who can't break down

In the middle of a work day

In the middle of the work week,

They need to save those moments

For the quiet shadows on Fridays

When you are home, alone

Because you never learned

How to make friends

And your age is betrayed

By the years heaped on your head –

When your body says twenty-seven

But your mind aches forty-eight.

And honestly, not having friends

Isn't completely a loss

Because being with them,

At some point,

Sooner or later,

You lose ways to relate to them

Because their walk of life

Is so different from your own.

I have often felt unimportant

And not worthwhile,

As though everyone already knew

Everything there was to know.

Everyone knew me, they knew everything

YOU SAY YOU KNOW ME

WHEN'S THE LAST TIME

THAT YOU SPOKE TO ME?!

WHEN'S THE LAST TIME

THAT YOU CHOSE ME?!

I CAN ONLY RECALL

BEING USED FOR FAMILY DRAMA

OR USED FOR VALIDATION

AND WHEN I WAS TIRED

OF BEING USED

I WAS LABELED A BITCH

AND HARASSMENT

BECAUSE YOU FUCKING KNOW ME

DON'T YOU?!

And now, I'm just angry.

I often feel taken for granted.

Maybe that's my own fault

I've become so good

At this façade of wellness,

So good *I* even believe it

And maybe that's why no one notices.

I have often felt subjected,

As though my pain was connected

To seven other beings

And because of this,

I can never speak freely

Or express what I'm feeling

Because being the oldest,

By default, makes you the strongest.

Maybe that's why no one can notice

And no one will ask me

And so few will love me

The way I need to be loved

And I am ashamed that it hurts me

Because I do not want your pity

This whole rant is not an expression

Of self-pity or misery

I don't want to hear that you're sorry –

I just wanted someone to choose me

When I was just a child

In an abusive world that forgot me.

And lately, I have chosen to choose myself.

I choose my Link to another world

Because this one I've been trapped in

Is demolished buildings and dust
And I have beaten myself up enough.
If no one will choose me,
I *will* choose myself
And the rest can go to hell
Because I am worth knowing *for me* –
Not for what I can do for you
Not for what you can do *to* me –
I am worth knowing
Because I am the strongest,
And I am worth loving
Because I am the kindest.
You just never knew it.
You just never knew me.
I have always felt forgotten
But today is a new day
And I have my Link to a new world,
And it's time for me to sleep.

I Am...Woman?

I cannot be as you –

I never was and never shall

For heartbreak has severed the love affair

Betwixt me and mine.

In some ways it is as divine

As throwing yourself from a cliff

Not knowing how you come back from it.

How do we measure a woman?

By the fruits of her womb?

By the treasures of her tomb?

And what makes a woman

When she is tortured and barren?

I cannot be as you –

I never was and never shall.

Eccedentesiast

I bite down hard on my tongue,

Blood seeps and mingles with regret.

Why do I do this?

Suffering in silence so others thrive.

But it's just a lie.

Or is it?

To tell the truth, I've forgotten it

And I'm fairly certain

I never knew truth to begin with.

I loosen my grip as I slowly slip –

I'm falling.

Do not catch me.

I will learn to fly

Or

I will simply die.

And for some reason,

I smile.

Ten Years

Ten years, I tell her.
Ten years ago, your mother
Was just a figure in a nightmare
Painted blues and dripping blacks
With red stripes across her back
Stitches in her mouth
To keep from spilling secrets
From the shroud
She wore across her naked heart
Beating frenzied in the dark.
Stone cold and solid
With a weight around her neck
Praying for the end
Watching for the end
Smoking gun held to her head
Eyes closed, wishing she were dead.
Ten years is a long time
But sometimes
It is still not 'fine'
Still, ten years is a long time

But sometimes I forget to cry.

I sigh and breathe out some memories

Tangled spiderwebs of lies we weave

Decaying husks of anxiety

Revived, temporarily

And as the dust settles around me

I notice they are words.

Without thinking, I begin writing

Replacing words like 'dying'

With lighter words like 'trying'

I would be lying if I said I understood it

All at once.

Ten years ago,

I was a little girl lost reading

In fairytales just dreaming

That someone would love me.

Maybe even want me.

Ten years ago was a long time

And more and more I can say it's fine

And mean it.

There are fewer and fewer secrets

When we write 'freedom'

And believe it.

And maybe someday

My pen will run out of ink

And I will not have to think

If it has been ten years or twenty.

The Cry

In the beginning,

Tears flooded the atmosphere

A new world was born

Trauma

My body burns.

It's 1 a.m.
And I'm afraid to go to sleep
Because the secrets that I keep
Have a way of popping up in my dreams
And it stings.
Yes, it burns.
My eyes are heavy
And heavy eyelids can't lie
But mine will try
Even as I deny this insomniac poetry.

My body burns.

I should be exhausted.
I spent my day working
And then went walking
And walked three miles
While my trauma was stalking

I've tried outrunning
But it's so damn clever
And if I turn to look back,
It gets busy creating
Pits for recalling
And walking turns to falling
And stinging
And burning.

My body burns.

After walking I came home and did some eating
Healthy and wholesome
Which transformed into exercising
And I worked my body
Till it burned inside me
Like *it* burns inside me
And my sweat was just
My body deeply crying
And for forty-five minutes
I kept reminding:

No one is going to hurt you.

Let go of this extra weight.

It's not a shield.

Not anymore.

I should be exhausted from this day,
A day of fighting and of trying -
Of coming to terms with and addressing.
But I still have trouble sleeping
Because

My body burns.

In Response to Your Question

I wish I didn't feel like this.

The skies are blue

And the wind is cool

And the sun looks so beautiful.

But somehow, today,

All I really feel is pain.

They say blue skies are blue

Due to the reflection of the ocean

And I wonder what my soul

Must be reflecting

For it to feel this way today.

I walk unjustified for not

Feeling happy,

Like the world is judging me

Because it provided me with beauty

Which I traded for my misery

As if I had a choice;

As if I woke up today and decided

I *wanted* to be miserable.

As if I wanted to be

Suppressed and pained.
What a history of taking
And no giving –
Of life stolen before living.
And my head aches and I look away
From the quizzical faces
Surrounding me, asking the predictable:
"Are you okay?"
And I'm left stuttering because
What is there really left to say?
When I've said a hundred times
"I don't know."
When I've expressed a thousand sounds,
Echoing in my soul
That pain takes me, and pain hurts me
And I have no say, either way,
I just have to hope that it will pass
And I will breathe
And that when I wake up,
The sky will be blue due to the
Reflection of the ocean
And my soul will finally
Reflect something different.

If I Had Friends

Hello friend, how's it going?

How's life?

How's it moving?

How am I? Oh, I'm sorry

My depression must be

Showing

Because I'm feeling pretty

Crappy

And this pain I have keeps

Growing,

And I'm busy counting

Worry

When I really should be

Sleeping.

What's that? Oh, I'm sorry

I didn't mean to come across

As needy

There's nothing you can do,

Just pretend you didn't

Hear me

Screaming

In the darkness

When the door was locked

Behind me

When you left and kept on

Walking

Leaving without looking.

Okay, okay, you're right –

It's been a good talk

It's been enough talk.

Maybe. Maybe later

We can take a walk into

My nature

It's mostly cloudy and rainy

But I swear to you,

There's beauty

If you look behind the

Shadows

In the corners of the

Framework

I build to keep my mind up

. While I avoid the echoing

'Time's up!'

Don't worry about the

Foundation

I'm great at the creation

Of walls in comparison

To windows.

It's funny but I

Haven't

Quite

Figured out those

Gardens! Let me show you!

I've planted acres of dewing

Poetry

That blooms in bitter

History

And feeds off of the moonlight.

What's that? Yeah, you're right.

It's probably too much

For you to take in

So, you take off as I close in

And I bolt the door behind you.

I bolt the door behind you.

I've got to get to tending

All the blossoms you were

Crushing

As you walked careless,

Without looking.

And these walls are filled with

Handprints

Because you touched them

Without asking

And now they're dirtied up with

Longing.

But hey, it's not your fault

I invited you without

Thinking.

Not everyone can love a broken heart

Or broken mind.

I should have known better

Than to hope

You'd love mine.

In the meantime, I will

Sterilize

All the feelings that you

Brought inside

Bacteria to a heart,

Deprived –

What's that friend?

Oh.

You're gone.

Goodbye.

Oh, To Be Cruel

I wish I could be heartless -

If at least for a moment

Return pain for pain, shame for shame

Release this anguish simmering

Under my scarred skin

Rage engulfing my veins,

An apocalypse waiting to begin.

I wish I could be cruel intentioned

Take what I want, manipulate the world I live in

Revenge deliberate abandonment -

And yet - I can't.

And truly, I would not wish

To be a harbinger of destruction

So I douse the fires of rage with the tears of my

tsunami

I remember that her name is grief

And it is not retribution that I seek.

It is recognition. Acknowledgment.

It is love.

And so, I weep.

Looks Like Rain

Luminescent liquid leaves my eyes
- there is no hope left -
Painted, parted, purple lips lie
 - of course, there is hope left -
Anguish addled asking heart cries
- then why do I feel like this -
Slumbering sadness soulfully replies
- rain is necessary for growth -

Burdens Come in Many Sizes

What a heavy weight is sorrow -

Bones lie heavy beneath skin,
Without will to move again
Thunderous cries rendering lungs
That succumb to violent gasps
And heartbroken rasps.
Hands clinging, desperately,
To wet sheets drenched in
Torrential tears, tsunami storming.
Grief swallows and I fall, plummeting
Hitting shallows of endless nightfall
And all the world dims,
Filled to the brim with my desperate call.
Limbs broken, body shaken
And the stars have departed my eyes
As I lie pinned beneath heartbreak.

- what a heavy weight is sorrow.

Sleep Is for The Innocent

At 11pm my head hit my pillow
I breathed in deeply
While I daydreamed about you.
At 12 am I tried reading a slow book
I read and re-read words
Without taking a closer look.
At 1 am I went to the bathroom
And thought maybe my bladder
Was the real demon.
By 3 am I entered the witching hour
I closed my eyes shut
But could not find my sleep power.
At 4:30 am I swallowed some pills
My husband slept soundly
But I just felt ill.
At 5 am he stirred in his sleep
And I cried for the rest
That I could not keep.
Sometime after 5:30 I finally slept
But insomnia creeped into my dreams

So I woke at 6:30 and once again wept.

Vulnerability

"It was one of the worst times ever," I breathe.

"Tell me," She says quietly.

Suddenly,

I feel as though I am standing

Alone and naked

With a heart near breaking

And I am terrified

That she will hear me

That she will see me

That I will open my body

And show her these scars

And that she will not understand me.

But I am here, and I am begging

"Please, please," I scream.

"Please tell me that I am worth

This vulnerability."

Please tell me that I am worth something.

"Will this hurt forever?" I ask her, painfully,

Oceans brimming tearfully.

"No." She says, determinedly.

"No, it doesn't have to."

Who Will Love Me?

What have I done?

Allowing myself to love –

Allowing myself to fall in love.

Foolish child.

No one wants you.

Who could love you?

Only those you've fooled.

Hear My Heart Call...Again

Hear my heart call
I know you heard it once before,
You didn't know what was in store
When you followed me there
To the place where my heart lay,
Vulnerability bare.

Hear my heart call
Could you love me as such I am?
A marked and broken man
You know that all I crave is love
I just want to be wanted,
Below or above.

Hear my heart call,
You tried to steal it like a thief
But I've laid waste to hands of grief.
I possess an angry and bitter soul –
A lust for love that leaves me cold...

Dearly Beloved

Dearly Beloved, we are gathered here
To rend this spirit from this flesh
And to lay to rest this wicked sin
Breeding beneath this skin.
Bless this unholy union of water and flame.

We call upon the spirits to tame
The lust riddled sickness seducing
The Bride of Christ.
It is with great shame we raise our blades
In a bloody sacrifice.
Pray, child, open your eyes
As we reclaim a body consumed by lies.

Much as he maimed me,
So did religion.
That was the last time
I prayed for redemption.

The Bleed

One quiet nook

Was all it took

And no one knew

And no one looked.

Insomnia

Now I lay me down to sleep –
Got you! My fevered brain is kidding,
While swirling thoughts defy my bidding
And set up counsel to keep sleep ridding.

Some look like dragons, some like snakes
But all are demons created by day
With dagger teeth and tails that sway
To the rhythm of Worry's drumming flay.

Worry is a creature bred from my bones
He's a gruesome thing and my brain is his home
But the veins to my heart are his telephone
And he mingles with Regret on his bloody throne.

Regret batters my heart through and through.
He prods the veins that make my blood run blue,
Whispers bad nothings whilst shines the moon,
And dances to Fear's deadly dirge tune.

Fear is a hazy, smoking black beast
Lurking in my stomach is his late-night feast
He laughs at my imperfection to say the least
And reminds me of the last time I tried to be free.

Last but not least, we can't forget Cold
He nips at my feet and bruises my bones.
No matter the cover, my body he roams
He's been here so long, he's befriended my soul.

Yes, now I lay me down to sleep
And meet the demons that I keep
And greet the thoughts that I keep
And let the darkness lull my dream…

The Build

Clocks tick in the background
And I am surrounded by an uneasy silence
Something like inner violence
Simmering in my veins
- I can't remember my name -
I close my eyes and remember
A September that felt much the same.
Around me, voices scream, demanding
Reprimanding all my undone deeds
Balancing his and her needs
Feeling ever so inadequate
- and he begs me not to quit -
But numbness creeps over my bones
And I don't know how to get through this.

Empathy

And sometimes,

I just hurt

For all the people

Around me.

Their emotions

Cascade like waves,

Drowning me

Delicately,

With an unspoken

Tragedy.

Forlorn, My Love

I wonder if I will ever feel

As though I am not on the run,

Burned up by the sun.

Running from the next heartbreak,

Running to the next sunset,

Begging love to stay

When it has already made its exit…

Scorpio

Sometimes I think it easier not to exist,
To let this slip of existence just...vanish.
I think of this heart people love to break
And of this smile I've been conditioned to fake.
How family and friends speak of promised love,
But splinter spines to bathe in blood.
How, in the end, I am always breaking,
A sacrificial virgin marked for the taking.
But the worst is in knowing I am worth nothing
Once drained of usefulness after the cutting.
And I label my pain as "scorpio dramatics"
For loving is pain and I'm lost in the statics.

I Swear I'm Not Crazy

Things that keep me up at night:

Did I pay that bill online?
Are *all* the doors locked?
Or did I forget the screen door?
How much milk do we have?
I wonder if dolphins dream.
I wonder if horses dream.
I wonder if, when dogs dream,
Do they dream about us?
Why does everyone hate me?
I wonder if he meant 'it's fine'
Or 'it's *fine*'.
Maybe I didn't smile enough.
Oh man, I bet I looked like a bitch.
I was trying to concentrate
But I think they interpreted that
Frustration as irritation and ego.
Why does everyone hate me?!

Does everyone really think

That everything's fine?

And really, what's the definition of 'fine'?

You say 'fine' and you mean it,

I say 'fine' and hope you'll believe it.

Does my brother blame me?

Secretly I think he resents me,

Just a little bit –

I mean, he'd probably never admit it

I've got plenty of things

I'll never admit to

Or did I just admit to that?

Does everyone believe I'm just

Another narcissistic flake?

A lot of people seem to fall off the grid

I'm still not sure if it's something

I said or something I did,

Who am I kidding?

It's probably both.

Oh my God, what time is it?

I cannot take *another* sleeping pill

And sleepy time tea seems

To have no effect on me –

Maybe I actually have a superpower!

I can live on no sleep and

My bones vibrate on demand!

If trees can communicate with each other

Through the sharing of energy,

I wonder if they listen in

On the energy created by my

Vibrating bones.

They vibrate a lot when I can't

Push back thoughts like

WHY DOES EVERYONE HATE ME?!

WHY CAN'T THEY SEE THAT I'M TRYING?!

WHAT CAN THEY POSSIBLY

WANT FROM ME

WHEN THEIR EYES ALREADY TAKE

EVERYTHING

AS THEY STARE AT ME,

SUFFOCATING ME,

WAITING FOR ME TO FAIL?!

Why does the wind shake the house

In a violent storm

And the lights *still* remain on 98%

Of the time?

I wonder what's wrong with mine

Since violent storms are on the rise

And my lights go out

Every.

Single.

Time.

When my vibrating bones

Reach their climax…

I wonder if birds have

Conversations about us?

Do they think our cars are

Sacrifices for their feces?

I wonder if thinking that makes me crazy.

Why does everyone hate me?!

I think about how I

Didn't say 'no' enough.

I replay all those times I gave up.

I hear a creak in the floor and think

Dammit! I forgot to lock the door!

But maybe it's the wrong door.

Maybe it's a metaphoric door.

Do dogs dream and if so,

What about?

I wonder if they dream about us.

If I go to sleep now,

I will get a whole four hours.

I will impress everyone

With an illusion of wholeness.

It *must* be a superpower.

What would my name be?

Insomnia Girl?

Well, that's pretty lame.

What about my motto?

Why does everyone hate me?!

It's weird that when

The wind shakes the house

In a violent storm

The lights remain on 98% of the time.

I wonder what's wrong with mine

Since violent storms are on the rise

And my lights go out

Every.

Single.

Time.

I wonder.

What is wrong with mine?

What

Is wrong with me?

I wonder

If thinking

Is the new

Sleeping,

These things that

Keep me up at night.

In Remembrance Of...

I cannot give you what you want -
Alone and lost in darkened thoughts.
Masked with smiles and endless grace,
You will not see my tear-stained face.
You will not see these shaking hands,
The whimper as I try to stand,
Red rimmed eyes and puffy skin
Or the desperate call to wake within.
You will not see this consuming sadness
Until it is too late...and I have left us....

Shhh . . .

Hush little Ravven, don't say a word –
Someone is listening and you can't be heard.
Hush your mouth and dry your eyes
Nobody here wants to see you cry.
And if you think you'll run away,
You're a foolish girl – you're here to stay.
Your bottled anger and your grief
Will steal your life like a diamond thief.
You'll push away all the ones you love
While you beg relief from the Lord above.
Listen to me, your closest friend,
Depression is here to hold your hand.
And don't believe the words they say –
Therapy never works anyway.
Hush little Ravven, don't say a word.
Pick up the knife, be a free little bird…

The Bleed

Bleed out my fear,

Let it curdle in the skin where I lanced it.

Let it pour down my arm where I felt it.

Let it come from my soul where you touched it.

But it's maddening!

And these scars are multiplying,

Each time I black out

From pain so excruciating

But there's nothing I can do

To stop myself!

- help me! help me! -

I'm bleeding out my fear

Like I heard I was supposed to.

To take control of this pain,

That's what I should do.

For if pain is all I have to

Look forward to,

Then I'll make my own pain

Just to spite you.

But I hate this, and I hate you

And I hate all the things you made me do!

- I hate this body, who it belonged to -

I'm bleeding through this broken skin

Because my broken soul is wearing thin

And blood reminds me that I am real.

- but I hate it -

Some say it's for attention,

Or an unhealthy fascination.

What do you know?!

Who are you, anyway?!

If you can't take this pain away

Then I suggest you take your opinions

And go to hell!

- I hate this, don't you know -

It's my only form of control.

- control -

You don't know how long I lived underneath it,

How many times I prayed that God would take it,

How many nights I held my breath

Hoping I would stop breathing.

- just stop, stop breathing -

- please, I don't want to keep living -

112

And still I kept breathing and living,

- *merely existing* -

Unable to depart for the sake of other hearts.

I have bled out my fear and I am weary.

I wear scars on my heart and now on my body.

- *there must be another way* -

Can't I be more than this?

- *am I worth more than this* -

I am captivated with the idea of something better

While my stained red skin is getting wetter

This time from tears, not from blood.

I am in torment, can't you see?!

And I hate this

- *I hate me* -

- *I just want to be free* -

I'd like to exchange this misery

And I'll put the knife down for a fee.

- *help me* -

I want to keep living.

A Thousand Cuts, A Thousand Scars

I cry out to you, a song of a thousand wounds

A thousand cuts on skin, ruined,

A thousand sins sleeping beneath my skin

An infectious fire burning me up within

As my quill turns bloody.

- please, won't you hear me -

We make light of dark poetry.

I use metaphors of moonlight

And flowers that bloom at midnight

A haven for all those broken and weary

- you don't know what he did to me -

And I write magic into my history

Trauma lending itself in entirety.

Hear me when I cry, for there is ink in the skin

And there is blood in the water

And I cannot falter.

And now there is blood in my pen

As I scribble 'pain' into 'poem'.

Cathartic blood-letting, ever so sanitary

And the poem produced unwinds masterfully

Not even a hint of tears cried in secrecy.

But I have cried over the scars in my art,

Memories and emotions from a battered heart.

We call it dark poetry and handle it lovingly

- you don't know what was done to me -

But somehow, in some way, there's less pain in my veins

Curiously, less anger attached to my name

And I think it's because it's been bled onto the page.

If there was blood magic, it would be dark poetry.

Wicked words wielded ever so carefully,

Power arises from the horrors done unto me

And I imbue it into the rhymes before you

Bleeding poems that scream ugly truths

You might have been broken but there is more to you.

I cry out to you, a song of strength and redemption

Behold my trauma which colors my poems

It takes a poet's pen to soulfully hold them

It takes a poet's pen to finally free them.

The Death

She writes of promises, broken

Each word a heartbeat, stolen

Each wound a blossom, open

Lonely Ghosts with Heartbeats

And I wonder if all we are

Are lonely ghosts with heartbeats

Spirits haunted with

'What if's' and 'could be's'

Unearthly projection

Of the labels that we seek

Caught between worlds

Who we are, who we would be

what they told us to become

Who we idolized to be

For sometimes I do not know myself

Or the reflection that I see

Smoldering dreams in liquid eyes

A past so dead, it can't be...

And I wonder if all we are

Are lonely ghosts with heartbeats

Destined to wander, lost

Till we decide the answer to

"Who are we?"

Welcome To My Graveyard

"How many graves?" she asks me
But in truth, I do not know.
Some are buried so very deep
And lay sleeping far below.
I only walk among them
As nameless as they are;
Unspoken, shameful tragedies
That haunt me from afar.
I can feel their presence in the wind
For the air is cold and stale
The leaves crumble beneath my feet
And the moon is wide and pale.
I can hear them whisper soft my name
As I pretend I can ignore,
And I walk among these gravestones
As if I too, had life no more.
I would wish to leave them flowers
Maybe then they would find some peace,
They'd be more than haunted spirits,
Perhaps they'd find that sweet release.

The lock on the gate is rusted
I'm not sure if it's to keep me out or in
But there's no lock in all the graveyards
To contain such an evil sin.
The shadows fall down across me
I think, they cannot see me now
But the dirt gives way beneath me
I am falling, I grasp anyhow.
I look down at this grave they dug me
I know they believe I was dead
But you can't kill what was never alive,
If you say that it's all in my head.
I unwire my jaws to speak freely
But God, how it does hurt!
I pull it out slowly and firmly
And I throw it down into the dirt.
There's blood seeping down from my cut lips
A tongue at last free to say
"You have stolen my past and my present,
I will not be silenced today."
I walk lonely among these old headstones
Broken and fragile with doubt
I hope to leave them all flowers

And smash the lock on my way out.

Hush Now,

And hold yourself, darling

Hold yourself, darling

While you move through your mourning.

Stop now,

And love yourself, darling

Love yourself, darling

As you cry for the morning.

Hey now,

Don't hate yourself, darling

Don't hate yourself, darling

While all your emotions are unfolding.

Hush now,

And hold yourself, darling

Hold yourself, darling

As you move through your mourning…

Laundry Day

It is frustrating

To be blind sided

By articles of wear

You thought you had discarded -

Cloaks of invisibility

Laces knotted with anxiety,

It's no wonder you can't see me

For the insecurities

Reflecting in this mirror

Screaming at myself

"Why can't you let go?"

Learning to Swim in The Middle of An Ocean

I breathe.

I tell myself,

'It's not hard to let go,

It's not hard to let show

The depth of this silence.

I know, you equate silence with violence

And I'm so sorry.

Just…breathe.'

In grade school, they said breathe.

Relax. Let your arms be like spaghetti,

Let your legs be light and unsteady,

Let go and you will float.

I apply this to my heart.

I apply this to my eyes

And suddenly, where I was paralyzed,

There is now a river,

There is now a lake –

There is now an *ocean*

As waves of emotions

Pour from a soul

That never learned how to tread water

And now must not falter

In the face of an ocean.

I breathe.

I can feel myself floating,

My body supported by these tears.

Aware of my fears,

I take a breaststroke

And pray that I won't choke.

I breathe as I settle into uncharted emotions,

Learning to swim

In the middle of an ocean.

D.O.A.

I have visited your grave but a thousand times
As I search for answers in these desperate times.
Broken lines, cobwebbed shrines,
Poetry divided by endless lies.
And I have tried to look past them
And I have tried to excuse them -
But you have gone and died despite them...
Your headstone is broken
Like the timeline inside me,
Fractured like memories
That lie in wait haunting me.
Much like you haunt me -
As my lack of existence still taunts me.
Murderous intent, applicable to both flesh
And the soul,
A DOA transcript left full of holes.
I caught a glimpse of the autopsy once:
Missing parts, broken hearts,
While foul play rolled away on the cart.
And these hands -

Oh, these hands,

They are covered in blood.

No glove is enough

When the truth is undone.

Oh graveyard,

I've visited you for a thousand times

Seeking comfort to bury a thousand crimes

Haunted whispers in a fragile mind.

Corpses waiting for a claim,

Trauma left without its name.

Stains on innocence rendered null and void,

A body tortured and destroyed.

I have watched your grave

For a sign of life

But if I look too close,

All I see is mine

And this grave is open

And this grave is deep

Deep

Deep

For these secrets that I keep

This grave is deep

And it is calling me.

Dear Little Rayven

"Do my dreams come true?"

"Yes, but not in the way you think they do.

You'll trade your happiness for survival

Until even breathing becomes a trial

And you'll lie and say that it's okay

Even as you walk in numbered days."

"But my blood, they appreciate me?"

"Oh, no, no they don't sweet baby."

Her eyes are brimmed in liquid sadness

"Will he love me? Does that ever happen?"

I close my eyes and inhale sharply,

"No, no he doesn't love you either,

And it will be a long time before it is easier

And you'll be hurt, so terribly

Before you have a chance to be much happier."

"But I will be happy?"

"Yes...eventually."

"Will you always defend me?"

Her words hang in the air, expectantly.

"No," I reply softly, "No, instead I treat you horribly.

For a long time I will despise you

And I will do everything I can to silence you.

I will smother you in scars and screams

And I will pray for your breathing lungs to cease.

I won't know how to love you

Until I meet someone who knows your value,

And sometimes, I will hurt you

On purpose, just to pull through.

You're going to feel broken

And so worthless and so pained

But that's how you discover love

And adopt your brand new name."

"I don't want to live through this!"

She cries, sobbing loudly in my ear.

"I know. But I promise, it will be worth your tears,

Because one day, you will wake up

And find so much fire in your belly.

You will find the strength to walk

Even as your legs shake and feel like jelly.

You'll put down the knife, you'll bandage up your
scars,

You'll find the wondrous magic of your loving heart.

You'll even make it through some therapy -

And I promise you, you'll come out okay
You will be loved and you will be happy."

I dry my tears and smile softly.
I am now loved.
I am now happy,
And I thank the child that survived inside me.
I'm sorry I did not love you
But the truth is I did not know how to
But I promise, it was never once about you...
And the thing I love most about you
Is the love you gave out so freely
For that is the truest essence of me
And despite all the hurt and harm done to me
No one
No one
No one
Can ever take this from me.

Forgive Me...

So busy taking care of hearts,
Patching holy lives and broken parts.
- Forgive me, Father, for I have sinned -
A smothering sickness thus begins.
Regret slumbering in a bottomless pit,
Vibrational anxiety causing fits,
- Look, we all knew she was crazy -
Depression misdiagnosed as lazy.
Angry, on fire, consumed with hellfire
- Screaming in a cage, "I am not a liar!" -
Grief flows through poisoned veins,
- Just let me loosen bloody rains -
Forgive me, Father, for I have sinned
Crucify me once again.
Blood-stained sheets and crusted wrists
Tear-stained journals, check marked lists.
Have no fear, it is just a scar
And I'm too tethered to go very far.
- Can you just hold me until it's done -

This is just a nightmare on the run.

Sweat soaked sheets and heavy breath

- Get your shit together, don't be a mess -

I am strong, alive, cannot be done in,

- Forgive me, Father, for I have sinned -

Kindling

I'm watching clouds pass by,
A thunderstorm on the horizon
And I catch myself wondering
How long the burning
Will linger this time
In veins that never sleep,
In blood that wants to seep
- if I could have just a little bit of pain
Maybe then I'd remember my name -
And I breathe in the electricity
Of a life continually in battle
With seasonal catastrophe.
- hush now, it's almost over now
Just hold on a little bit longer -
I warn him, "Put the knives away
Until this feeling passes away."
It isn't that I want to,
It is that I am obligated to
And sometimes death seems better
Than the burning in my skin.

- take a breath and begin -

The clouds pass by and the sky clears

As inner fears melt into twilight.

I breathe out once again

A crackling sensation on my skin

As the spell is broken

And once again the words are spoken

- I've made it this far,

Too far to give in -

I forget in these moments of trauma

How far I have come within them

Without them,

All around them,

Because I am more than them

And they are but a small part of me.

The lights may dim

And my skin may burn

Because I am on fire

And I know,

I am not the only one.

I Am Sick That You Remember

I pause to ponder the words you bring to mind.

They would be words like:

Ghastly. Terrible. Demented. Evil. Vile. Disgusting.

Despicable. Putrid. Bile.

There is no kindness in my heart for your existence

No forgiveness for this life I've been forced to

witness,

And I hope that when you finally pass into the next

life

The only mourning occurring will be the amount of

time

You existed to begin with.

And if I ever have the displeasure of seeing you again,

I will mark your presence as yet another sin

May God have mercy on your soul.

So choke on this tasty piece of truth:

From me, there will be no redemption for you,

There is no love or remembrance of it for you

And I pray to God you die alone in a cell

And remember me as the woman who condemns you to hell.

The Transformation

Wicked words haunt me

You are not enough for me

Fire in my palms

148

Because Love Is Hard to Master

Dear Link,

I'm feeling particularly poetic,

I don't know how to show it,

So here goes it:

You illuminate my shadows,

You create dimension inside my chaos,

Which leaves me at a loss

For an excuse to just exist.

When I think I've lost my way,

I remember you are what home is

And where you are, I will be.

When I am with you,

I am the person

I was always meant to be –

A girl with a heart and

Halloween vampire fangs

Waiting for the boy

With the apple cheeks

To come over and say hello to me,

Which you did!

And my heart was in your hands

The instant you said:

"Nice teeth!"

You've taught me tripping is okay

And it's safe to fall into love, into arms.

When the darkness creeps around me,

I remember you are what hope is

And I have hope in what we can be

And where you are is where I'll be.

You bring out all those cozy thoughts –

A house, a child, a little puppy,

Growing old and sipping tea

In the apple trees.

I love you,

And you love me.

Really, that's all I could

Ever hope for,

Because love is hard to master

So much give and take

But I have learned it's okay to

Give and take

When your arms are no longer

Chained

To a hopeless fear of yesterday

But rather your arms are draped

Across the shoulders of

A likeminded soul

Who also looks for love

And shelter from the cold.

When I am afraid to move forward,

I remember you are what courage is

And I will brave any moment

To be with you

And stay with you.

You are what love is

And I love you

And you love me

And that is all I could ever hope to be.

Bloom

I find that life tends to bury me.
I find small, everyday choices
To be *overwhelming*.
Small stresses become
Huge burdens
Because they remind me
I am not quite altogether.

Every time I make my way
Through waves of endless bodies,
I absorb the emotions
Of a hundred nameless people.
I feel their sadness and their joy,
Their desperation and their fear
Because I happened to catch their eye
And noticed that their eyes
Were like mine.

Some people call empathy a gift.
To me it is neither gift nor curse.

Being open to a vast expanse of emotions
Means taking it for all it's worth –
Whether that means a cold rebuttal
From the masses,
A warm welcome of familiarity,
Or the crushing pressure
Of being smothered and covered
In lonely grains of emotions
Drifting on the current,
Wanting and waiting for
Validation and reconciliation.

I find that life tends to bury me.
I find it hard to keep up with
Friendship and the following maintenance.
My lack of normalcy separates
My continuity from everyone else's.
I cannot speak of childhood or history
Or how I even came to be –
Born around twenty-three.
For that reason, I am distant
And awkward
And *so* unsure.

And people find that to be
Uncomfortable.
I *do* understand their point of view
But who I am is who I am
And if that bothers you,
You have every right to choose.

PTSD and anxiety sometimes
Conflict with each other.
PTSD reminds you that you don't care
And anxiety reminds you that you should.
PTSD struggles to care for the mundane
While anxiety causes you to question
Every. Little. Thing.

I find that life tends to bury me.
I take solace in my garden,
Growing life where once
Grew nothing.
Cultivating energy and beauty,
Calmness and tranquility.

Some time ago,
I planted poppies
In remembrance of my father.
This morning they had still
Not surfaced
And I feared I had smothered them too deep.
This evening as I watered,
I saw my first tiny leaf
Pushing through the dirt,
Growing, in spite of me.

I find that life tends to bury me.

I find it worthwhile to bloom
Like a deeply buried poppy.

And I will bloom,
In spite of me.

If My Heart

If my heart was an insect,

It would be a beetle.

I would wish for it to be a butterfly,

But I have found it better

To be covered in skeleton

Than in powder.

If my heart was a flower,

It would be a sunflower rather than a rose –

Because I do not require pain or suffering

In order to love me

And I will always follow the sun.

It is easy to write nonsensical comparisons

About this heart of mine

Each line a fun little gesture

To a much deeper matter

That I just cannot say.

There is a reason I write poetry.

They say I need to tell my story,

Bare my heart and my history

But instead I scribble poetry

That is messy with metaphors

And adlibbing with adverbs.

But poetry is well and fine

When I am the one writing it.

Sometimes I forget that not everyone

Knows my heart

And that my heart is poetry.

A phonetic symphony,

Words that express without the brutality.

Not everyone knows this,

And neither should they.

But sometimes,

When the messages pop up on my phone,

I will startle and brace myself

Because I know

There will be no poetry to ease me in gently.

And you may not believe this,

But my own story still startles me.

I write poetry not just for you

But also, for me.

It is hard for you to hear,

It is hard for me to say.

Sometimes I feel guilty for sharing

Because what I have to say is poison –

It makes you feel sick

But it is killing me.

My poetry is like

Medicinal poultice.

It eases the pain and pulls it out of me.

There we have it,

More poetic comparisons

But this poem is for me

And for me alone,

Because my heart is poetry

And I *love* poetry!

It bespeaks beauty and passion,

Grief and chaos,

It is a beautiful creation of great traumas, of great

loves,

And of great victories.

If I could choose one thing for my heart to be,

It is this.

Sometimes I just wish

That if people are to think of me,

They would speak in poetry

Because I am so much more

Than unmetered prose history.

This Is Where the Healing Begins

Last night I ventured out onto the water.

I spoke to the moon in whispers grown louder

As I cried out for my father -

For someone, to remind me I am stronger

Once in a while, my days just feel longer.

Around me, glittered waves broke on stones

As I sighed and rested my broken bones,

A desecrated temple decorated in headstones.

I cried for a heart that has fallen in love

And I watched the stars emerged far above

As a bird with clipped wings who doesn't belong.

But the moonlight was soft as it lit up my way

I felt myself blossom as tears dried on my face

And I knew, in my heart, that I would be okay.

The wind kissed my curls, caressing my brow

The waves lulled my heart with their gentle sounds

And for a moment, I felt my feet leave the ground.

I danced along the pier, completely alone

Embraced by a darkness that only I know

Safe. Free. As though I was...home.

There's something to be said for a recharge at night

When the heart and the mind just can't get it right,

When one wants to fly but cannot achieve flight.

And I still don't have answers for my whispered secrets

But I know the moon doesn't mind, she will keep it

For a darkling who saves her tears for the darkness.

For a heart that still loves.

And still hopes.

And dreams all of it.

Dragons Make Kind Companions

Firestone eyes smolder upon me

Liquid loveliness burning fiery

Unmatched splendor

Swathed in starlit wonder

A golden heart beating

Welcome for the taking

If only I could be

If only…

Nobody

Nobody loves someone
The way you love me.
What I should say is:
Nobody loves someone like me
The way that you do.
Nobody loves someone like me
The way that you do.
I have to say it twice
Because it takes time to sink in.
Love was not a prize that came cheap.
Love was an endless fight
To prove I was good enough,
Except I was never good enough
And 'good enough' was
Being Jesus.
And I've nailed myself to crosses
Only to come back scared and scarred
Because I couldn't save the masses
And I could not save myself.
Jesus is perfect.

Jesus is good enough.

I can never be Jesus,

Therefore, I could never be

Good enough.

Somehow, we always

Seemed to miss the fact

That at the end of the day,

Jesus is love

And his love is good enough

For all of us, for everyone.

So, if 'good enough' is love

Why wasn't I good enough?

Why wasn't I loved?

Asking myself these questions

Brings me to the same conclusion:

Because nobody loves someone like me.

Not only was love withheld from me,

I was persuaded that when

Someone told me they loved me,

It was a lie to abuse me,

To use me and to take all

That they could from me.

So, in summary, I was not

Good enough,

And love was a lie.

I must go back to my

Original statement:

Nobody loves someone like me

The way that you do.

It took me years to learn

That 'love' and 'abuse'

Were not interchangeable,

That love is Jesus

And Jesus is perfect

And there is *nothing*

Like perfect love.

I call you 'nobody' because

I was taught you did not exist.

So, how true it is that

Nobody loves someone like me

The way that you do.

You love me like Jesus,

So, in your eyes, I am good enough.

And I am loved.

I'm sorry, Jesus,

But I think I was taught wrong.

I am someone,

And I *am* good enough.

Nobody loves someone like me

The way that you do.

Fever Dreams

I'm breaking through barriers

Leaving smoldering corpses

Of fevered dreams behind me.

I built myself a portal

With my Link

To a new world.

And I'm leaving,

But I will never forget.

Ever The Outsider

I watch from the outside, peering within
Wondering why I cannot fit in.
I've worked really hard to master projection
Yet always end up alone with rejection.
And rejection is no kind companion at all -
A nasty little fellow who laughs when I fall.
So I bandage my heart, keep it close to my chest
Straighten my shoulders and shrug off the rest.
In the end, it's okay, I prefer to be free,
And I don't fit in because there's no one like me.

𝕱𝖚𝖈𝖐 𝖄𝖔𝖚

I will never forget the words

You spoke behind my back

You thought I could not hear

Perhaps you just did not care,

So flippant with the weight your words would bare

for years.

"Why is he with her? She's so much bigger than him!"

Snickers caught in an unforgiving wind.

Link didn't hear you but I did.

You will never know the pain inflicted

By words so wicked

A body bruised and broken

Traded as a token

A body I did not know how to love,

Sacrificed, bloodied, scars waiting and at the ready

And all you noticed was that I was heavy,

And what a God forsaken tragedy

That a woman might be curvy.

"Why is he with her?"

Somehow, it hurts harder when inner fears are spoken
by another,

For I had thought the same thing:

Why he stayed with me, why he loved me

For I was nothing and I had nothing

And I was tired and downtrodden

From the anguish that had been done to me.

But oh, he loves me!

He loves every inch of me!

And he knows how to hold the weight of me

Physically, spiritually, emotionally.

And it's funny how when you're loved right

Weight practically disappears overnight.

I saw you yesterday and you did not acknowledge me,

Only Link beside me and for a moment I froze

Trapped in your hateful words from years ago

But I stood up straight and looked you in the eyes

And I smiled because I realized:

You don't matter.

I am going home with Link whose heart is so much
bigger than you

And you, well, you'll be going home, alone.

And I wish I could say I could be the bigger person
and forgive you
But, surprise!
I'm not as big as I used to be.

Words

And I pick myself up
And I dust off the words
You tried to stick me with,
Cause I know words are words –
Angry little vowels
And conscientious letters
Surrounded by derogatory question marks
And accusatory exclamations.
And at the end of the day,
I remember words are power
- but only power if you believe them -
So I pick my vowels and my letters
And I stick myself with my own word:
Strong.
And I am strong.

𝕾𝖊𝖑𝖋-𝕻𝖔𝖗𝖙𝖗𝖆𝖎𝖙

Eyes that have seen too much

And have so much more to see.

Wrinkles beneath that support

The baggage that was never claimed.

Skin that dries in winter and sweats in summer

With pores the size of caverns

Because I never learned the difference

Between dry and oily

Kind of like how I never learned

The difference between fine and angry.

Shoulders that sport some scarring,

A collarbone that used to sport sapphire bruising,

Arms that have carried worlds and broken hearts

And so much emptiness,

But that's why I have muscles –

To carry both my children.

One to whom I said goodbye

And one who makes me feel alive.

A chest containing a platinum ribcage

To protect a heart that beats beyond its age

A fragile flutter of years.

A stomach that's soft from neglect and fears,

That's marked with hope

In the form of stretch marks

That follow the story of my character arcs.

A uterus that has known pain and joy

And fear, nine months of it

As it fought to secure a future.

Hips that can make a man stop

Or a woman for that matter

Though I always labeled them bigger and fatter

Legs that have walked miles and miles

And made miles seem shorter

Because I grew stronger.

Feet that have walked on eggshells

Until I decided to crush them

Until I decided to demolish them

And that's when I started running –

Building legs that could run so fast and so hard

Until I was so far

Healing a uterus that deserved love

And a stomach that could steel itself

In the face of anything

A chest that could withstand anything

A heart that could love anyone!

Arms that could protect anyone,

That could hold everything!

Powerful arms that could cradle infants

Or punch with the swings!

A collarbone that straightened my shoulders

As I straightened my resolve

As I learned how to love!

I learned how to perceive

Weaving a thicker skin

That could still be soft.

As my eyes really learned to see,

A self-portrait.

Two ways I see myself:

The half that was broken down

And the half that rose back up.

And I honestly think it's kind of beautiful

Something that could not be recreated

Something so real because I have *lived* it.

A masterpiece.

Cracks and all, scars and all

A portrait of disaster and success

But mostly of love that made the most of it
And that's how I want to see myself
Even if no one else can see it:
A body that didn't give up
That will never give up
That will run till the end of it.

Easy, Now

One foot in front of the other,

One minute at a time.

If the days feel heavy,

Just carry the minutes.

Haunted and Holy

(Father, forgive me for I have sinned
And my heart is breaking apart within
They say I'm wrong, they say I'm bad
That every fault is mine to have —)

Father, crucify me, render and undo me
Father, can you tell me why truth is so contemporary?
Why Biblical chapters translate uncertainties
But stoic absolutes trump all of my questioning?
We accuse each other of picking and choosing
As if my birth was a choice of my doing
As if I had a say in the DNA construction
How brown my eyes are, how my lungs function
How long my legs grow, which brain side I use
The way I filter in colors, how much weight I can
lose,
If my immune system is strong or predisposed to
illness
Where my talents lie and how I find fulfillment,

If I gesture like my mother but speak like my father,

If I have curly hair like my maternal grandmother.

Such foundation based inside our unique creations

But when its matters of the heart, there are no
deviations

There's no room for difference, step in line, bow our
head

If you're not coming out straight, then you're better
off dead.

Father, forgive me, but how have I sinned?

How am I wrong for the love that I give?

Condemn me with verses out of context, out of line

"But love is the greatest of these" left behind.

I wonder at the beginning; how many were like me?

And when Jesus walked among us, where was his
speech on sexuality?

We base our truth in texts translated according to the
day

Trace it back far enough, what does it really say?

There are over 30,000 verses in this holy book

Hundreds speak to salvation, redemption and hope

Hundreds more on social justice, on caring for the
poor

And Jesus' greatest message was to love each other
more.

And in these thousands of verses, *five* are used to
condemn

Five are mistranslated that homosexuality is a sin

Or any variant of that – bi or pan or ace

Polyamorous, transgender, anything that isn't
'straight'.

Out of *30,000* verses, *five* are used to abuse

Each translation a contradiction labeled as the truth.

Father, forgive me for I have sinned

By letting the masses abuse me again.

If love is your message, I must be touched by divinity

Because love is my core, and love is what rules me,

And when you created me, you granted me
unconditional compassion

And instead, for myself, I've allowed deep seated self-
hatred

And I think that must pain you, for I am your
creation.

Father, forgive me, for I have sinned

By denying divinity, forgetting that love always wins.

But

I am sorry Father, for these things I must say:

You gave me strength in the darkest of days
But days turn to mourning and searching and doubt
I find faults in the logic of what You're about.
As a teen, I never thought that my faith would falter
But too much is demanded to become your daughter.
"God has a reason, He has a plan."
Where was your reason when I was raped by that
man?
When I was starved and abused, and covered in
bruises?
"Everything works according to His plan if He
chooses."
And maybe it's just humans who twisted who you are
Either way, this has left me with a terrible scar.

Thank you for the comfort you brought me when I
was alone
But truth be told, Father, I was never welcomed in
your home.

I'm not sure what I believe, I still think you are real

But there has to be more in the longing I feel.

I have to let go if I am ever to heal.

I didn't come out 'straight'

And I deserve to feel real.

Coals

I am forlorn,

A heart draped in silence and

Bittersweet whispers.

I don't know how to let go

When I don't remember

Holding on.

- could you please just hold me

until the fires subside within me

I am lonely

I am lonely

I am

lonely -

Burning Quills

I have been told I have the heart of a poet,

With a pen spilling words that consistently shows it,

A knack for blending pure hope into fear

A rope at the ledge when the ending is near,

A light in the darkness to show you the way

A promise that there will be better days,

Sometimes disgustingly optimistic -

It's just in my blood, you know I can't help it.

I like to believe I write magic from darkness

That I can save the dark ones lost among us.

I like to believe I can bring hope to this world,

A Darkling Queen birthed from a scared little girl.

I like to believe I'm worth more than my past

That the 'then' and the 'now' is a sharp contrast,

But it's hard to believe and it's hard to push on

When a voice deep inside screams that I'm wrong.

Just a matter of time until everyone knows

The thing I'm most good at is just a big show!

I dare think I'm someone - I'm not even real!

How can I speak truth when I don't know how to
feel?
I don't belong among true clever creatives -
I'm a fraud, I'm a sham, and full of self-hatred.
Who do I think I am?! What have I done?!
Dreaming big dreams with a heart on the run.
Imposter syndrome simmers deep in my mind
Leftover trauma from a past far behind.
A chaotic battle between who's wrong and right
And just one of the shadows creating my night.
I don't write this for pity, I write for awareness
For those who also have thoughts that betray us.
Do you think you're nothing, a joke, or a sham?
Well then you'll fit right in so come take my hand.
We mustn't let fear control our potential -
It's time to view life from a different angle.
So I'll take my pen, and yes, you take yours
And we'll do what we do weaving our words.
In times when I'm overwhelmed by this voice
I'll remember these words amid all the noise:
I have been told I have the heart of a poet,
With a pen spilling words that consistently shows it.

Phoenix Fire

Today I rise on wings of sorrow
Casting ashes of tomorrow
What I thought life would be
Hoping my future will now fly free...

The Sun

And like a Phoenix,
I will rise from these ashes –
Death, where is thy sting?

The Dawning

Spring peepers have arrived

And I smile for the first time in a long while.

A sliver of moonlight kisses my face

As the wind caresses every place

It's been such a long, long winter

The warmth of remembrance unthawing my bitter

Is this ...what it means to be alive?

I trace my lips where the moon has kissed

Eyes closed in silent forgiveness

I have waited so very long for this.

I breathe frost as I exhale,

Crystal shards dissipating without fail

And into my lungs I welcome life.

And I think, this must be what it's like to be alive.

Perhaps it would be okay to cry

Release these rivers cascading memories

And give birth to a new sanctuary

One where spring peepers can sing peacefully.

Is it possible to live in Springtime always?

Blossoming promises blanketing green days

I settle silently, allowing the earth to move through me
And I awaken alive learning healing comes seasonally
But for now, I am alive amongst the spring peepers singing
And I tremble, overwhelmed by moonlight intoxicating
And I think, as tears spill from starry eyes
This...this must be what it is to be alive.

Here We Are

Not the same as yesterday
Won't be the same tomorrow.
Stronger than my illnesses,
Conqueror of sorrow.
Healer of all brokenness,
Warrior of pain.
Carrier of faithfulness,
Owner of my name.
Left the past behind me,
My baggage on display.
No shame for me to carry
As I choose to live today.
Champion of broken hearts,
Mental pain, and fear.
Not perfect by a long shot
But confident and real.
Don't waste your tears upon me
And do not try to give me shame
I may have once been broken,
But I will never be, again.

How to Eat When You're Sad

I eat when I'm sad.

I have depression.

I engage in a persistent battle

With my depression,

Therefore, I always carry

Some shade of sadness.

So, if I'm always sad,

And I eat when I'm sad,

Well, you can see

Where this is going.

I eat when I'm anxious.

I have anxiety.

I'm not constantly anxious

But when I am,

Oh, my lord!

You'd think the world was ending,

If you could feel my bones vibrating

And hear my palpitations pounding,

You'd probably be closer to understanding.

Those moments require

An extra handful of shame,

An extra mouthful of disappointment.

In the beginning, there was cutting.

Cutting was pain, but pain I could control

In an environment where pain

Was clothing I was forced to sew and wear.

Instead of necklaces,

I wore suffering around my neck.

My ears sported some very piercing

Verbal abuse

And my wrists maintained

Only the best of the bruises.

Cutting came with control

And control became another

Kind of apparel.

But I didn't wear my control

On my wrists,

I wore it on the places

Upon which I carried the most:

My shoulders.

And then I met someone.

He cried over my scars

As he bandaged fresh wounds

And I told myself, if this was love,

If this was love,

I couldn't scar him too.

But vices don't disappear overnight

And control was an adornment

I was not willing to sell.

I found comfort in food

Because food didn't leave scars,

It was more socially acceptable,

And 'fat' became a word

I could hide behind easier

Than a doctor's note

Labeling me as a compulsive cutter.

Food didn't ask me if I was

Really hungry

If this pit of 'empty'

Was in my stomach or my soul,

If I was just sad.

I eat when I'm sad.

I also love when I'm sad.

I realized one day that love

Was stronger than sadness

Because in the middle

Of a really bad day,

I found myself laughing

In the face of my sadness

As his fingers were woven with mine

As we walked in the sunlight.

I bottled my tears and I said to my fear:

"These are tears of joy

And they do not belong to you!"

I eat when I'm sad,

But I'm getting better.

My depression banks in

At just over 300 pounds,

But I find that love and happiness

Is a choice that carries

So much more weight.

I will swallow the good moments

So, they are still digesting

When the bad times come.

I'll devour all the love I can consume

Because it's healing my insides

Better than any cheap liquor

Or store-bought sweetness.

I'll savor the laughter

When his fingers are woven with mine

As we walk through this life

Whether it's rain or sunshine.

So, I still eat when I'm sad,

But love is the best diet I could find.

I highly recommend it.

Ideally, I'm talking love for yourself,

But if you're like me and

You find it hard to love your reflection,

Love someone else.

And trust me,

I stepped on the scale this morning

And saw my depression weigh less

Than it ever has.

This is what you do when you're sad:

Take care of yourself

So when the good times come,

You can be alive in the moment

And not be held back for

One. Single. Minute.

This is how to eat

When you're sad.

I'm Over It

I have decided to stop apologizing for my existence.

For eating chocolate,

For wearing shirts three sizes too large for me

Because I am ashamed of the space

I take up with my body.

I won't apologize for my anxiety

Or my depression

Because as long as

I don't wield them as weapons,

They are no one's business.

I have decided to stop being

A half-stitched garment

Of someone else's choosing.

I'm not going to drown in this suffering.

I'm not going to cave to the overwhelming.

I'm done apologizing.

Except to myself.

Move On

I woke up one day with bloody wrists
And saw the sun had forsaken me
Alone in the dark with no one there
What kind of life was this to be?
I healed, I fought, I wanted more
Although I did not know what more was.
All I knew is that I longed to be held
To be wanted, to be free, to have love.
But as I said, growth is scary and difficult
So I hid behind labels and trauma
It was easier to accept I was a broken thing,
Forever hanging on semi colons and commas.

But it was never enough and I needed more
So I paused on the brink of desires.
I allowed myself hope and a will to believe -
I allowed my cold soul to catch fire.
I dabbled in trust and learned how to give
And I fell into love with my life.
I'm so very grateful for the day I chose growth

Instead of choosing the blade of the knife.
My trauma did not mold me into who I am
I did that all on my own,
By learning to love, learning to trust,
Learning how to build my own kind of home.

It's never too late to grow and to change
You just have to make the right choice.
What is your life worth? How about your love?
Are you willing to claim your own voice?
If I can choose to be more than my trauma,
If I can be more than my pain,
You too can give up the ghost of the past
And step out into the light of your name.
I've created a world for those just like us
People who just don't belong in the sun.
Put down the heartache encasing your life
It's time for you to move on...

Gardens

Growth can be exponential
When we allow it in our lives.
Growth is an active choice,
Be it subconscious or otherwise.
Sometimes our brains have had enough
And they're ready to close some doors,
Then it's our choice to listen up
And let go in order to have more.
Don't get me wrong, it's scary
And can be painful along the way.
Sometimes we are bullied for who we are
Sometimes the night is longer than the day.

I Chose to Stay Alive

The snow is falling, and I look tenderly around

At this new life that I have found

Things I never thought I would have

When I was fifteen and nineteen

A little girl trapped in uncertainty

Warped by trauma and abusive tendencies

And I think of the time I wished for death

I prayed for death

I prayed for God to end my misery

Notebooks full of suicidal maybes

A body bruised in brutal captivity

And I'm so glad, I'm so glad

I chose to stay alive.

So, What Will It Be?

When the light comes to greet you,

Will you welcome it with love?

Or will the darkness come to claim you,

And what will it remind you of?

Two sides to every story,

Two halves to every soul.

So, will the light now be your savior,

Or will the darkness take you home?

Stay

I feel like you need to know
That you are not worthless.
That the sum of who you are
Allows not for specific purpose
But rather, to encompass everything.

I think you ought to know
That you are not loveless.
That you will be loved in different ways,
There's no need to be nervous
And you are very much worth loving.

I would wish for you to know
That you are allowed to be gladless.
That you are allowed to let emotions exist,
You are not required to fake happiness.
Acceptance gives way to healing.

I want so badly for you to know
That you are so very much more than this.

That grief is a timeless companion
That intertwines beautifully with forgiveness,
Encouragement to keep growing.

I feel like you need to know
That you are not worthless.
- You are not worthless -
And you are much more than this.
I hope you hear what I'm saying.

Here's to The Broken People

The world will know you
The way that I know you.
And the world will love you
But only at a fraction
Of how they *should* love you.
But they *will* know you
Because I will tell them.
Here's to you,
My beautifully broken people.
We are all one and the same,
Lives bonded over pain,
Our lives struck by tragedy.
We have learned that pain
Does not discriminate
And we are all at its mercy.
We walk with cloaks of trauma
To shield our battered hearts.
We speak in words of wisdom
That can only be spoken
By a broken heart.

We live our lives in mirrors,

Caught in reflections

From our past.

We fear our future is but an echo –

Happiness fades, and it fades fast.

We have swallowed grief

By the gallons

And smothered out our own voice,

We are told to be afraid

And that we do not have a choice.

We see darkness in the light,

We hear echoes in the song,

You say we have been through hell,

But hell has *just begun.*

We are estranged from

Things like happiness, security and peace.

You cannot fathom what we'd give up

For a day without anxiety.

Here's to my broken people,

You are the salt of this earth.

You may not believe it,

But your lives are filled

With purpose and with worth!

You have a power no one else has!

You are a reckoning in the bend!

You are the hope of our generation.

You are. You *are!*

You are here, my friend.

Do not let the hurt consume you,

Do not let the depression win,

You are strong and powerful –

Look at you! Standing in the end.

And when your burdens

Feel quite heavy

And your hope has fallen

Far below,

Remember we are sisters

And we are brothers,

And we will *never be alone!*

Here's to my broken people!

Let me hear you shout out loud!

Do not stand among the shadows,

Own your pain and wear it proud!

Because you are more than

What you came from,

You are more than

What's been done to you!

You are hope's incarnation

Simply because...you are you.

Here's to the broken people,

Like me, like you, like them.

You will give me a reason to speak up.

I will give you a reason to stand.

For the Poets Before Me

I look back at the poetry

That inspired me as a child

And I smile

While I read them.

I see most of them were

About lost love,

Adventures and romance

That magical first glance,

And of course, death.

Death and travesty,

Broken hearts for the bounty –

Solemn prose with hidden meaning

I am sure I did not understand –

And still they spoke to me.

Still, they were captivating,

This inner pain of poets before me,

Who made death and trauma

A heart wrenching romance,

Spilled ink meant just for me.

For their pain, I felt empathy,

And I *felt* their feelings,

Though at the time

I didn't understand the reasons

Why death and trauma

Whispered sweet nothings

Through prose and poetry –

Careful words that spoke

Much more than dark woods

On a snowy night,

And love lost in a kingdom

By the sea,

And a girl called nobody

Named Emily.

Such beauty in pain.

Depression never looked so lovely.

But depression and trauma

Were not things understood

At twelve or fifteen.

They were not words in my

Vocabulary

And I did not really know

Why these lines meant so much to me.

And now, at twenty-seven,

I read them line for line
And I realize why they
Belonged with me,
Why I felt such empathy.
Why I felt they were written for me.
I thank the poets who came before me
For the influence on a girl
Who went to the library,
Weekly,
For the sole purpose of
Checking out stacks of books
Full of poetry.
Thank you.
In my world of suppressed emotions
Your words were buckets
Of oceans
Of all the things I felt inside,
All the darkness I had to hide,
And I may not have
Understood my trauma,
But your prose changed my life
And a period
Became a comma.

You introduced my very first pen,

My sword, my defense.

A new way to begin.

My chaotic emotions

Transformed into poems.

I hope my poetry can be

Half as good as yours.

I hope someone reads my words

The way I *devoured* yours.

I hope someone reads them,

Maybe not understanding

But feels kinship and

Longing

Because my words are

A reflection of their heart,

Either whole or just a part,

And they know they are not alone.

I hope I make their load

Worth carrying.

For the poets before me,

Thank you.

Cry of the Corvids

You there with the familiar face –

You echo lost love and a broken place.

Do you look to belong, a haven, a space

To exist and to heal, disappear with no trace?

Then come, join my murder and my unkindness,

We take the worst of the pain that would bind us

And transform it to a beautiful shelter of darkness,

And here you can rest and be loved in like-
mindedness.

Put down the knife, the rope, and the gun –

Any weapon that renders your dark life undone.

You are not alone; you need not live on the run.

My Curious Corvid, do you feel out of place in the
sun?

We have all been there and together we thrive.

So come, take a step into this, the dark side.

You've heard of the shadows on walls, intertwined?

I send them to stop you on the night you would die.

They come up as poetry and birds of jet black,

They pull at your heart as you question your act,

"If someone has lived in spite of all that,

Then maybe this ending is not where it's at."

So come, join my Darklings, we promote health and growth.

We encourage your life when you need it the most,

And you won't feel alone since we live among ghosts.

We change the world with kindness and poetical posts.

There are gardens to lounge in with moonlight to relax

And don't worry of questions, for we will not ask.

I promise, there's more to your life than the past –

So come, take my hand, embrace life and new paths…

A Word

If you or someone you know is struggling with suicidal thoughts, self-harm, depression, anxiety, or anything in between, please seek and encourage professional help.

There is so much life to be had.

I promise.

My Unkindness

Link – thank you ever and always for loving and supporting me as I change and grow. Nothing seems to phase you and it is a comfort knowing you are always there. I don't know what I would do without you. You are everything. It is hard to believe we have been together a decade. Perfection never looked so lovely. I love you more than love.

Starlight – I'm not sure you will ever read these but if you do, please know everything I have done has been for you. From the moment I saw you on the monitor – a tiny little egg sac! – I knew you would change my world. And you have. And you continue to do so. You challenged me to break cycles I didn't think I had the strength to. I want the world for you, my love, and the beauty that comes with it. I love you more than love.

Peridot – From the moment I met you, I knew you were someone special. You have opened my life to pieces of the world I never knew existed and you've opened me to pieces of myself that I didn't know were allowed to exist. You are so special and important to me and you have changed my life in unfathomable ways. Thank you for everything you have done to support me and CCP. I couldn't have done any of this without you. I love you more than love.

Awaken

What if Ravven wasn't as she seems?

What if her story held magic?

Did you find the hidden messages?

Did you read between the lines?

Who is exactly is "*Ravven*"?

- The Lore of Ravven -

Coming soon…

www.ingramcontent.com/pod-product-compliance
Lightning Source LLC
Chambersburg PA
CBHW030412130626
46549CB00004B/1745